Published By Nicholas Thompson

@ Darren Chilson

The Plant Paradox: Recipes to Nourish Your Family

Using You Lose Weight, Digestive System, Easy Plant

Paradox

All Right RESERVED

ISBN 978-87-94477-45-1

Table Of Contents

Stuffed Mushrooms

Ingredients:

- Vegetable oil

- Eight ounces of cream cheese (softened)

- fourth cup of parmesan cheese (grated)

- fourth tsp. of each

- Onion powder

- Black pepper (ground)

- Twelve whole mushrooms

- tbsp. of each

- Minced garlic

- Cayenne powder (ground)

Directions:

1. Preheat the oven to 175 degrees Celsius. Grease a baking tray with the help of cooking spray.

2. Clean the mushrooms using a damp kitchen towel; break the stems. Chop the mushroom stems finely.

3. Take a skillet and heat oil in it. Add chopped stems of mushroom and garlic—Cook for five minutes.

4. Remove the skillet from heat and let it cool. Add the cream cheese, black pepper, parmesan cheese, cayenne powder, and onion powder. Mix well.

5. Use a small spoon for filling the mushroom caps with the mushroom stuffing.

6. Place the mushroom caps on the prepared baking tray.

7. Bake for twenty minutes until liquid forms under the mushroom caps.

Tomato Brochette

Ingredients:

- fourth cup of olive oil

- 3 tbsps. of balsamic vinegar

- third cup of basil

- fourth tsp. of each

- Black pepper (ground)

- Salt

- baguette

- 7 tomatoes (chopped)

- 1 cup of sundried tomatoes

- 4 garlic cloves (minced)

- 3 cups of mozzarella cheese (shredded)

DIRECTIONS:

1. Preheat your oven on the setting of broiler.

2. Combine tomatoes, olive oil, vinegar, garlic, sundried tomatoes, basil, pepper, and salt in a bowl. Let the mixture sit for ten minutes.

3. Cut the baguette into slices of a 4fourth inch. Arrange the baguette slices on a baking tray. Broil for 3 minutes until browned.

4. Add the mixture of tomatoes on the slices of bread and top with mozzarella cheese.

5. Broil again for five minutes.

Spicy Pumpkin Seeds

Ingredients:

- 3 tsps. of Worcestershire sauce

- 3 cups of pumpkin seeds (raw)

- 3 tbsps. of margarine

- 1 tsp. of salt

- eighth tsp. of garlic salt

Directions:

1. Preheat your oven at 135 degrees Celsius.

2. Combine the INGREDIENTS: in a mixing bowl.

3. Bake for hour. Stir in between.

Sweet Potato And Pumpkin Pudding

Ingredients:

- 1 tablespoon of maple syrup

- 1 teaspoon of cinnamon

- 2 tablespoons of pumpkin puree

- 1/3 cups of rolled oats

- 1 large cooked sweet potato or yam (baked)

- ½ cup of soy or almond milk

Directions:

1. Mix the entire INGREDIENTS: listed above in a blender until it has a smooth consistency.

2. Serves 23 and takes only 10 minutes to prepare (not including baking the yam, which can take up to hour).

Sweet And Sour Rhubarb Yoghurt Parfait

Ingredients:

- 2 cups of coconut yogurt

- 2 teaspoons of maple syrup

- ½ cups of chia seeds

- 1 cup of blueberries

- 1 cup of stewed rhubarb

- ¼ cups of rolled oats

Directions:

1. To prepare the rhubarb, slice 23 stalks into inch pieces before adding in a casserole full of water.

2. Let it start boiling before adding in 2 teaspoons of maple syrup, then reduce in heat and continue to cook on medium until

the rhubarb is soft. Remove, drain, and rinse, then place in a bowl to be chilled for almost 1 an hour.

3. In a large dessert cup or sundae glass, scoop the rhubarb to the bottom of the cup, then top with several scoops of coconut yogurt, swirling in the maple syrup, then top with the chia seeds, blueberries, and rolled oats.

4. For best results, soak the chia seeds in coconut milk or yogurt of 3 hours before adding to this recipe.

Brownie Cake

Ingredients:

- 1 cup of cocoa powder of baker's chocolate

- ½ cup of coconut oil

- 1 cup of water

- 1 teaspoon of baking powder

- 1 cup of low carb sweetener (monk fruit or swerve)

- 1 tablespoon coconut flour

- 2 cups of almond flour

- Dash of sea salt

- 1 teaspoon of vanilla extract

Directions:

1. Mix all the dry INGREDIENTS: in a large bowl and set aside. Prepare the oven by setting it to 350 degrees.

2. Pour the following items into the bowl with the cocoa, flours, and sweetener: water, coconut oil, and vanilla extract.

3. Blend thoroughly, then pour into a lined or greased baking pan, and bake for 2530 minutes.

Raw Orange Chocolate Pudding

Ingredients:

- 1 cup pitted dates

- 1/3 cup raw or regular cocoa powder

- 1 teaspoon of orange zest

- ½ cup of freshly squeezed orange juice

- 1 vanilla bean, seeds scraped out (or 1 ½ tsp pure vanilla extract)

- A cup of peeled, pitted, and roughly chopped ripe avocado

- 1/8 teaspoon of sea salt

Directions:

1. Combine all INGREDIENTS: in a food processor and puree until smooth.

2. You can thin the puree by adding more orange juice, or a splash of nut milk or water.

3. Serve or store in the refrigerator.

Mango Chia Seed Pudding

Ingredients:

- 1 teaspoon of vanilla (powder or extract)

- ¼ teaspoon of cardamom

- 1 medium sized mango

- 2 cups of coconut milk

- ½ cup of chia seeds

- 3 tablespoons of coconut nectar or 2 tablespoons of date paste

Directions:

1. Mix chia seeds with coconut milk, coconut nectar, vanilla, and cardamom in a bowl and refrigerate up to overnight.
2. Slice the mango up into pieces and puree in a blender.

3. Serve accordingly – mix together or serve in

    layers and enjoy!

Chewy Lemon And Oatmeal Cookies

Ingredients:

- ½ cup quick cooking oats

- ¾ cup roughly chopped walnuts

- 2 tablespoons of grated lemon zest (from about 2 lemons)

- 2 teaspoons of natural cocoa powder

- 1 teaspoon of vanilla powder

- ½ teaspoon of baking soda

- 10 dates, pitted

- A cup of unsweetened applesauce

- 1½ teaspoons of apple cider vinegar

- A cup of rolled oats

- A cup of oat flour

- Pinch of sea salt to taste

Directions:

1. Preheat the oven to 275°F and line 2 baking sheets with parchment paper.
2. Soak the dates in hot water for about 20 minutes then blend them with applesauce and vinegar.
3. Stir together the rolled oats, oat flour, quick
4. cooking oats, walnuts, lemon zest, cocoa powder, vanilla powder, baking soda, and salt in a large bowl.
5. Mix in the dates and applesauce paste and make sure that the mixture is relatively dry.
6. Scoop a portion, roll it into a ball, pat it flat and place onto a baking sheet. Repeat this until you use up all the mixture.
7. Bake for about 40 minutes until the tops of the cookies appear crispy and browned.

8. Let them cool on a wire rack. Enjoy.

Cacao Lentil Muffins

Ingredients:

- 60 ml water.

- 60 g raw cocoa powder.

- 120 g wholewheat flour.

- 20 g peanut flour.

- 10 g baking powder, aluminumfree.

- 195 g cooked red lentils.

- 50 ml melted coconut oil.

- 45 ml pure maple syrup.

- 60 ml unsweetened almond milk.

- 70 g Vegan chocolate chips.

Directions:

1. Preheat oven to 200° C/400° F.

2. Line 12hole muffin tin with paper cases.

3. Place the cooked red lentils in a food blender. Blend on high until smooth. Transfer the lentils puree into a large bowl. Stir in coconut oil, maple syrup, almond milk, and water.

4. In a separate bowl, whisk cocoa powder, wholewheat flour, peanut flour, and baking powder.

5. Fold in liquid ingredients and stir until just combined.

6. Add chocolate chips and stir until incorporated.

7. Divide the batter among 12 paper cases.

8. Tap the muffin tin gently onto the kitchen counter to remove air.

9. Bake the muffins for 15 minutes.

10. Cool muffins on a wire rack.

Chickpea Crepes With Mushrooms And Spinach

Ingredients:

Crepes:

- 5 g nutritional yeast.

- 5 g curry powder.

- 350 ml water.

- 140 g chickpea flour.

- 30 g peanut flour.

- Salt, to taste.

Filling:

- 10 ml olive oil.

- 4 portabella mushroom caps, thinly sliced.

- 1 onion, thinly sliced.

- 30 g baby spinach.

- Salt, and pepper, to taste.

Vegan mayo:

- 15 ml lemon juice.

- 5 ml raw cider vinegar.

- 15 ml maple syrup.

- 170 ml avocado oil.

- 60 ml aquafaba.

- 1/8 teaspoon cream of tartar.

- 1/4 tsp dry mustard powder.

- Salt, to taste.

Directions:

1. Make the mayo; combine aquafaba, cream of tartar, mustard powder. Lemon juice, cider vinegar, and maple syrup in a bowl.
2. Beat with a hand mixer for 30 seconds.
3. Set the mixer to the highest speed. Drizzle in avocado oil and beat for 10 minutes or until you have a mixture that resembles mayonnaise.
4. Of you want paler (in the color mayo) add more lemon juice.
5. Season with salt and refrigerate for 1 hour.
6. Make the crepes; combine chickpea flour, peanut flour, nutritional yeast, curry powder, water, and salt to taste in a food blender.
7. Blend until smooth.
8. Heat large nonstick skillet over mediumhigh heat. Spray the skillet with some cooking oil.
9. Pour 1/4 cup of the batter into skillet and with a swirl motion distribute batter all over the skillet bottom.

10. Cook the crepe for 1 minute per side. Slide the crepe onto a plate and keep warm.

11. Make the filling; heat olive oil in a skillet over mediumhigh heat.

12. Add mushrooms and onion and cook for 68 minutes.

13. Add spinach and toss until wilted, for 1 minute.

14. Season with salt and pepper and transfer into a large bowl.

15. Fold in prepared vegan mayo.

16. Spread the prepared mixture over chickpea crepes. Fold gently and serve.

Sweet Potato Toasts

Ingredients:

- 1/4 inch thick slices.

- 1 tbsp avocado oil.

- 1 tsp salt 1/2 cup guacamole.

- 2 large sweet potatoes, sliced into.

- 1/2 cup tomatoes, sliced.

Directions:

1. Preheat your oven to 425° F.
2. Cover a baking sheet with parchment paper.
3. Rub the potato slices with oil and salt and place them on a baking sheet.
4. Bake for 5 minutes in the oven, then flip and bake again for 5 minutes. Top the baked slices with guacamole and tomatoes.

Vegan Tomato & Coriander Pancakes

Ingredients:

- 400ml soya milk

- vegetable oil, for rying pan

- 140g white selfraising flour

- 1 teaspoon soy flour

For the topping

- 250g cherry tomatoes halved

- 2 tablespoon soya cream or soya milk

- sizable number pine nuts

- snipped chives, to function

- 2 tablespoons vegetable oil

- 250g button mushrooms

Directions:

1. Sift the flours along with a pinch of Salt into a blender. Add the soya milk and mix to create a smooth batter.
2. Heating Just a little oil in a moderate nonstick skillet till very hot.
3. Pour about 3 tablespoons of the batter to the pan and cook over a moderate heat until bubbles appear on the surface of the pancake.
4. Flip the pancake over with a palette knife and cook on the other side until golden brown.
5. Repeat with the remaining batter, keeping the cooked pancakes warm as you move. You may make roughly 8.
6. For The topping, heat the oil in a skillet. Cook the mushrooms until tender, then add the tomatoes and cook for a few mins.
7. Pour from the soya cream or milk and pine nuts, then cook till blended.

8. Split the sausage between 3 plates, then spoon on the berries and mushrooms. Scatter with chives.

Vegan Granola

INGREDIENTS:

- 150g dried apple, roughly sliced

- 150g coconut oil, melted

- 250g pack mixed nuts, roughly chopped

- 400g jumbo oats

- 2 tsp cinnamon

- 100ml walnut syrup

Directions:

1. Heating Oven to 180C/160C fan/gas 4. Line 3 large baking trays with baking parchment.

2. Mix all of the INGREDIENTS: together except the maple syrup. Spread the granola out onto the trays and drizzle over the maple syrup.

3. Bake From the oven for 20 mins, stirring the granola nicely 1way through so it cooks evenly. Leave to cool before storing it in a Kilner jar or airtight container. Best eaten within 1 month.

Mexican Beans & Avocado Toast

Ingredients:

- 2 garlic cloves, crushed

- 1 teaspoon ground cumin

- 2 tsp chipotle paste or 1 tsp chili flakes

- 2 x 400g cans black beans, drained

- little bunch coriander, chopped

- 4 slices bread

- 270g cherry tomatoes, quartered

- 1 white or red onion, finely chopped

- 1/2 lime, juiced

- 4 tablespoons olive oil

- 1 avocado, finely chopped

Directions:

1. Mix the berries, 1/4 onion, lime juice, and 1 tablespoon oil and set aside. Fry the rest of the onion in 2 tablespoons oil until it begins to soften.
2. Add the garlic, fry for 1 minute, then add the cumin and chipotle and stir fry until aromatic. Hint in the legumes and a dash of water, cook and stir gently until heated through.
3. Stir in the majority of the tomato mixture and cook 1 minute, season well and include the majority of the coriander.
4. Toast the bread and garnish with the remaining 1 tablespoon oil. Set a piece on each plate and pile a few beans on top.
5. Organize some pieces of avocado on top, and then scatter the remaining tomato mixture and coriander leaves to function.

Matka Smoothie Bowl

Ingredients:

- Ch tbsp chia seeds

- Oon spoon make powder

- 6 oz coconut yoghurt or Greek yoghurt

- 1 teaspoon greens powder (optional)

- Stevie to taste

- ½ teaspoon Gobi berries

- 1 teaspoon coconut flakes

- C tbsp cacao nibs

Directions:

1. Add the curd to the matka and mix. If you
   wish, add it to stevia to make it sweeter.

2. Empty the mixed smoothie in a bowl. Garnish
    with cacao nib, chia seeds, coconut flakes and
    goji berries.

Coconut, Avocado, Apple Keto Smoothie

Ingredients:

- 1 apple slice

- ½ tbsp collagen powder

- 1 teaspoon lemon juice

- ¼ cup non milk coconut milk

- 1 medium avocado, rinsed, peeled, and destined

- Ct spoon met oil

- ½ teaspoon chopped uncooked coconut for garnish

Directions:

1. Combine all INGREDIENTS: in a food processor and mix until smooth. Top with sliced coconut.

Blueberry Power Shake

Ingredients:

- ¼ cup Greek yogurt or plain yogurt

- ¼ cup fresh or frozen blueberries or blueberries

- Eas Spoon Pure Vanilla Extracts

- ½ tbsp virgin coconut oil

- ½ cup coconut milk

- 4 snowflakes

- Stevia to taste or any dessert you like.

Directions:

1. Add all INGREDIENTS: to a food processor.
2. Blend until smooth until frozen or ice fruit is mixed. Adjust sweetness if necessary. service tax.

Low Lection Guacamole

INGREDIENTS:

- 34 sprigs of cilantro and/or parsley

- black pepper, 1 tsp (fresh ground)

- Sea salt as desired

- 2 large avocados, raw and ripe enough to mash and mix

- ½ red onion or 1 small red onion, diced finely

- 2 teaspoons of olive oil

- Chili pepper, as desired (optional)

Directions:

1. Mash the avocados in a large bowl, then stir in the oil, sea salt, chili pepper, and black pepper.

2. Mix well, then add in the diced onions and

continue to mix.

3. Parsley and/or cilantro can be finely diced to

add into the recipe or added as a topping or

garnish instead.

Lectinfree Biscuits

Ingredients:

- Chestnut flour, 3 tablespoon

- Coconut flour, 1 teaspoon

- Almond flour, 1 teaspoon

- Psyllium husk flakes, 1 teaspoon

- Baking powder, ½ teaspoon

- Cinnamon, ground, 1 teaspoon

- Sea salt, ¼ teaspoon

- 1 egg

- Hy or maple syrup, or your choice of sweetener, 1 teaspoon

- Vanilla extract, 1 teaspoon

- Coconut or dairy milk, 4 tablespoons

- Olive oil or coconut oil, 4 tablespoons (extra virgin oil is recommended)

- Sorghum flour, 6 tablespoons

DIRECTIONS:

1. To prepare the oven, preheat to 300 degrees and line 3 baking trays with parchment paper or a silic mat.
2. Use a rolling pin to ensure the mat or paper is evenly lined.
3. Mix the flours, sea salt, and baking powder, then add the cinnamon and combine thoroughly.
4. Using another bowl, whisk the egg and combined the vanilla extract, milk, olive or coconut oil, and hy or maple syrup. Gently combine the liquid INGREDIENTS: into the dry, flour mix, and stir well to blend.

5. Use a spatula to ensure n of the batters sticks to the sides of the bowl and work the dough with your hands until it is formed evenly.

6. If the dough is too wet or sticky, add a bit more sorghum flour. If it's a bit too dry, add a splash of milk.

7. Add either of these INGREDIENTS: little at a time, until the desired texture is achieved.

8. Move the dough to a baking tray that has been lined with a silic mat or parchment paper, and use your hands to flatten the loaf, forming into a square or rectangular shape.

9. This doesn't have to be perfect, though you can form this shape as best as possible, making sure it is even in thickness all around.

10. On top of this dough, add a second parchment paper and roll the dough to just about ¼ inch of thickness, then remove the top paper, using the bottom sheet or mat to move the dough to the baking sheet.

11. Keep it on the bottom paper or mat and poke holes evenly spaced on the dough, to create the biscuit appearance.

12. Bake the biscuits in the oven for about 2830 minutes and observe them.

13. As the edges become brown or golden, they will be ready to take out of the oven.

14. Allow to cool. For best results, take the biscuits 1way through the baking process, about 1415 minutes, and separate or slice them into small, bite sized shapes.

15. This will allow the dough to cook evenly and thoroughly throughout. When the biscuits are d, turn off the oven and allow them to sit for an additional 10 minutes to bake in the residual heat, then remove them and allow to cool.

16. Enjoy them warm, or seal and save safely for 4 days. They can be refrigerated for up to week or longer.

17. These biscuits are delicious on their own, or they can be served with a nut based spread or butter.

18. They can be enjoyed with a cup of coffee or tea or prepared as sores for a campfire snack.

Gingerbread

Ingredients:

- ¼ cup of flour (lectinfree)

- Reship mushroom powder, ¼ teaspoon

- Dried, ground cinnamon, 1 tsp

- Water, tablespoon

- Butter or ghee, softened or melted, 2 tablespoons

- Baking powder, ¼ teaspoon

- Sea salt, 1/8 teaspoon

- Ground ginger, ½ teaspoon

- egg

- Vanilla extract, ½ teaspoon

- Monk fruit sweetener, 1 tablespoon

- Instant coffee powder, ¼ teaspoon

- Whipped cream (organic)

Directions:

1. Combine the dry INGREDIENTS: into a small bowl, whisking together thoroughly until they are well blended.
2. Add in the egg, melted or softened butter, vanilla extract, and water.
3. Continue to whisk until everything is smooth without any lumps.
4. Set the bowl in a microwave and heat for 90 seconds on high heat, or until the gingerbread rises to the top of the bowl.
5. Whip the cream in a separate bowl until peaks are formed. Pull the gingerbread mixture onto a plate or flat surface, then slice the gingerbread into 46 pieces.

6. Let the slices cool on a plate, and top with
    whipped cream, and top with a light dusting
    of cinnamon.

Plantain Pancakes

Ingredients:

- 2 teaspoons of pure vanilla extract

- 1/2 teaspoon baking soda

- 1/4 cup of xylitol

- 2 large green peeled plantains

- 4 large pastured eggs

- 5 tablespoons of coconut oil

- 1/8 teaspoon of iodized sea salt

Directions:

1. Puree the plantain using a processor or boil them and then smash them.

2. Add the eggs and blend to form a smooth paste.

3. Now you can add the vanilla, 1 of the coconut oil and the rest of the INGREDIENTS: until it is smooth.

4. Heat an extra tablespoon of coconut oil in a pan.

5. When hot, use ½ a cup measure and pour batter into the skillet.

6. Cook 5 minutes until the top is dry and has some bubbles, flip it and cook for another 2 minutes.

7. Repeat until you've used the entire mix.

Cassava Flour Waffles

Ingredients:

- 1/2 cup of melted coconut oil

- 1 tablespoon of hy

- ¼ teaspoon of salt

- 1/2 teaspoon baking soda

- 4 eggs

- 1/2 cup cassava flour (or tapioca flour)

- 1 package of frozen unsweetened wild blueberries

Directions:

1. Preheat a waffle iron.

2. Then, add the eggs, the flour, oil, baking soda, salt and hy (or sugar) to a blender and mix them until you have a smooth mix.

3. Using a 1/4 cup measure, scoop mix into the
    waffle iron and cook.
4. Then you can add some more hy and the
    blueberries.

Paradox Crackers

Ingredients:

- 1 teaspoon of filtered water

- 1 cup of almond flour

- 1/2 cup coconut flour

- 2 large pastured eggs

- 1 teaspoon of your preferred seasoning

- 1/2 teaspoon of salt

Directions:

1. Preheat your oven to 350°F.
2. Whisk the eggs and water in a bowl.
3. In another bowl mix both flours, the salt, and the seasoning.
4. Add the egg and blend with a spatula until you eliminate any lumps.

5. Form small marbleized balls and put them on

    a cookie sheet.

6. Press them with a fork and bake for 20

    minutes.

Chocolate Waffles

Ingredients:

For waffles:

- ¼ cup coconut flour

- ½ teaspoon baking soda

- ½ teaspoon organic vanilla extract

- ¼ cup 70% dark chocolate chips

- 1 cup blanched almond flour

- ¼ cup cacao powder

For sauce:

- 2 tablespoons coconut oil

- ¼ cup 70% dark chocolate chips

Directions:

1. Preheat the waffle iron and grease it.

2. In a mixing bowl, mix together cocoa powder, baking soda, flours, and salt.

3. In another bowl, add hy, vanilla extract and eggs mix well.

4. Add the egg mixture into bowl with flour mixture and mix well.

5. Gently, fold in chocolate chips.

6. Add ¾ cup of mixture to waffle iron. Cook for 5 minutes.

7. Repeat with remaining mixture.

8. For the sauce, in a small pan, add coconut oil and chocolate chips over low heat and melt while stirring continuously.

9. Serve the waffles with the topping of chocolate sauce.

French Style Crepes

Ingredients:

- 1 teaspoon organic vanilla extract

- Salt to taste

- 4 organic eggs

- ½ teaspoon ground cinnamon

- 2 tablespoons arrowroot powder

- 1 tablespoon olive oil

- 2 tablespoons almond flour

Directions:

1. In a mixing bowl, add almond flour, arrowroot powder, salt and cinnamon and mix well.
2. In another bowl, add vanilla and eggs and beat until well combined.
3. Add the egg mixture into flour mixture and mix well.
4. Using a nonstick pan heat the oil over medium heat.
5. Add the desired amount of mixture to pan to coat the bottom in a thin layer.

6. Cook for 1 minute per side.

7. Repeat with the remaining mixture.

Loaded Breakfast Muffins

Ingredients:

- ½ teaspoon oregano, dried and crushed

- 2 small garlic cloves, minced

- 2 tablespoons olive oil, divided

- ½ medium sweet potato, peeled and grated

- 1 cup fresh mushrooms, chopped

- 2 small carrots, peeled and grated

- Salt and freshly ground black pepper to taste

- 1 lb. grassfed ground chicken

- 1 small onion, chopped

- 8 large organic eggs, beaten

Directions:

1. Preheat your oven to 355°Fahrenheit. Lightly grease 12cup muffin pan.
2. Take large pan and heat 1 tablespoon of oil over medium heat and sauté onion for 5 minutes.
3. Add the garlic and oregano to pan and sauté for 1 minute.
4. Add the chicken, salt, black pepper and cook for 7 minutes.
5. Transfer the chicken mixture into a bowl.
6. Take your remaining oil and add to same pan and cook carrots and sweet potato for 3 minutes.
7. Place mushrooms into pan and cook for another 2 minutes.
8. Stir in some salt and pepper and cook for another 3 minutes.
9. Transfer the vegetable mixture into the bowl with chicken mixture and mix well.
10. Add the beaten eggs and mix well.

11. Add the mixture to prepared muffin tins.

12. Put into your oven and bake for 20 minutes or
    until they become golden brown.

13. Remove the muffin tin from oven and keep
    onto a wire rack to cool for about 10 minutes.

14. Carefully invert the wire rack and serve warm.

Super Nutrient Smoothie

Ingredients:

- 1 handful of chopped kale with stalk removed

- ½ cup blueberries

- ½ cup raspberries

- 1 cup unsweetened almond milk

- 1 spoonful of almond butter

- ½ a thumb size piece of fresh ginger skin removed and grated or minced

Directions:

1. Prepare and wash INGREDIENTS: as necessary.
2. Add all INGREDIENTS: to a blender and blend until smooth.
3. Pour into glasses and drink immediately.

Fruit, Nut And Seed Oatmeal

Ingredients:

- ¼ cup granola

- ½ cup mixed berries (Blueberries, raspberries, strawberries or acai)

- ¼ cup mixed nuts (Brazil, Hazelnuts, Pecan, Almonds, Walnuts, cashew, etc.)

- ½ cup steel cut or other oatmeal

- ½ cup almond milk

- 2 tablespoons mixed seeds (pumpkin, chia, flax, sunflower, sesame, hemp, etc.)

Directions:

1. To eat cold, add all INGREDIENTS: to a bowl and mix to combine.

2. To eat hot add the oatmeal and almond milk
    to a saucepan.

3. Heat through gently for a few minutes until it
    begins to thicken.

4. Remove from heat and place mix into a bowl,
    add the remaining INGREDIENTS: and mix to
    combine – eat immediately.

Vegan Breakfast Burrito

Ingredients:

- 1 diced fresh tomato

- 2 tablespoons of salsa (try making your own)

- ½ lime

- ¼ cup cilantro (chopped)

- 1 wheat or maize tortilla wrap (vegan)

- 1/2 cup refried beans (heated)

- 1 small avocado peeled, deseeded and sliced

- ¼ cup of sliced romaine lettuce

- Siracha hot sauce

Directions:

1. Use a toaster to warm the tortilla wrap gently.

2. Place the warm wrap on a plate and add the refried beans, avocado, lettuce, tomato and salsa.

3. Add a splash of sriracha hot sauce to taste and close the wrap.

4. Garnish with a squeeze of lime and some chopped cilantro.

5. Serve immediately.

Cinnamon Apple Coffee Cake

Ingredients:

For the cake:

- ½ teaspoon baking soda

- ½ teaspoon salt

- 1 cup plant based milk (such as soy or almond milk) ½ cup unsweetened applesauce

- ⅓ cup melted vegan butter

- 2 cups all purpose flour

- 1 cup granulated sugar

- 2 teaspoons baking powder

- 1 teaspoon vanilla extract

For the topping:

- ¼ cup granulated sugar

- ¼ cup brown sugar

- 1 teaspoon ground cinnamon 1 cup diced apples

Directions:

1. Preheat the oven to 350°F (175°C) and lightly grease a 9 inch round cake pan.
2. Mix the flour, sugar, baking soda, baking powder, and salt in a mixing dish.
3. In a separate bowl, whisk together the plant based milk, applesauce, melted vegan butter, and vanilla extract.
4. After adding the liquid comments, mix the dry INGREDIENTS: only until they are barely blended.
5. In a small bowl, combine the granulated sugar, brown sugar, and ground cinnamon for the topping.
6. Spread 1 of the cake batter into the prepared cake pan.

7. Sprinkle 1 of the topping mixture evenly over the batter.

8. Layer the remaining batter on top, followed by the remaining topping mixture.

9. Scatter the diced apples over the top of the cake.

10. A toothpick placed in the center of the cake should come out clean after 35 to 40 minutes of baking.

11. After the cake has cooled in the pan for ten minutes, move it to a wire rack to finish cooling.

12. Slice and enjoy this moist and fragrant cinnamon apple coffee cake as a delightful treat with a cup of coffee or tea.

13. Feel free to customize these recipes by adding your favorite INGREDIENTS: or experimenting with different flavors. Baked goods and pancakes are versatile, and you can have fun

exploring various combinations to suit your
taste preferences.

14. Enjoy the process of baking and savor the deliciousness of these homemade treats!

Mediterranean Quinoa Salad

Ingredients:

- ½ cup diced red onion

- ½ cup sliced Kalamata olives

- ¼ cup chopped fresh parsley

- 1 cup cooked quinoa

- ½ cup cherry tomatoes, halved

- ½ cup diced cucumbers

- ¼ cup crumbled vegan feta cheese (optional)

For the dressing:

- 2 tablespoons freshly squeezed lemon juice 1 clove garlic, minced

- ½ teaspoon dried oregano

- 2 tablespoons extra virgin olive oil

- Salt and pepper to taste

Directions:

1. In a large bowl, combine the cooked quinoa, cherry tomatoes, cucumbers, red onion, Kalamata olives, and fresh parsley.

2. In a small bowl, whisk together the olive oil, lemon juice, minced garlic, dried oregano, salt, and pepper to create the dressing.

3. Pour the dressing over the salad and toss until well coated.

4. If desired, sprinkle crumbled vegan feta cheese on top.

5. Enjoy this Mediterranean inspired quinoa salad as a light and flavorful meal.

Sesame Ginger Salad

Ingredients:

- ½ cup edam me beans

- ¼ cup chopped green onions

- 2 tablespoons sesame seeds

- 4 cups mixed salad greens

- 1 cup shredded red cabbage

- 1 cup shredded carrots

- ½ cup thinly sliced bell peppers

For the dressing:

- 1 tablespoon sesame oil

- 1 tablespoon freshly squeezed lime juice 1 teaspoon grated ginger

- 1 teaspoon hy or maple syrup (optional for sweetness)

- 2 tablespoons soy sauce or tamari

- 1 tablespoon rice vinegar

Directions:

1. In a large salad bowl, combine the mixed salad greens, shredded red cabbage, shredded carrots, sliced bell peppers, edam me beans, chopped green onions, and sesame seeds.

2. In a small bowl, whisk together the soy sauce or tamari, rice vinegar, sesame oil, lime juice, grated ginger, and hy or maple syrup (if using) to create the dressing.

3. Drizzle the dressing over the sale d and toss until well combined.

4. Serve this inspired sesame ginger salad as a refreshing and satisfying option.

Weight Cooked Lima Beans, Kale And Turkey

Ingredients:

- 1 pound dried huge lima beans, flushed and picked through

- 4 cups vegetable stock or b soup

- 3 cups water

- 2 teaspoons Italian flavoring

- 1 little fed bin turkey thigh, around 3/4 pound

- 2 tablespoons grainy mustard

- 2 teaspoons powdered sage

- Ocean salt, ideally iodized

- 1 pack Tuscan, dark, or other kale

- 1 medium red or yellow onion. cleaved

- 2 cloves garlic. minced, or 1/2 teaspoon garlic powder

- 2 tablespoons extra virgin olive oil or avocado oil

- Broken dark pepper

- 4 to 6 tablespoons extra virgin olive oil or truffle oil, for showering

Directions:

1. Cut the leaves off the stems of the kale. Cleave the stems and slash the leaves into bigger parts. Put in a safe spot. If your weight cooker has a saute element, sauté the onions and the garlic in the oil for around 5 minutes.

2. Then again, sauté them in a non Teflon skillet or wok over medium heat. Move the garlic and onions to the weight cooker. Include the vegetable stock and water. Include the beans, Italian flavoring, and turkey thigh.

3. Cook at high weight for 14 minutes, then
    enable the strain to descend normally. Expel
    the turkey, and mix in the kale leaves,
    mustard, sage, and salt and pepper to taste.
    Shred the turkey and come back to the pot.
4. Mix until very much mixed, and spoon into
    serving bowls. Sprinkle each presenting with a
    tablespoon of olive oil or truffle oil.

Altogether Modern Millet Cakes

Ingredients:

- 1/4 cup cleaved carrots

- 1/4 cup cleaved basil

- 1 cup cleaved mushrooms

- 1 clove garlic, cleaved

- 1/2 teaspoon Italian flavoring

- 2 tablespoons extra virgin olive oil or perils oil

- 1/2 cup millet

- 2 cups vegetable stock or water

- 3/4 teaspoon ocean salt, ideally iodized

- 1/4 cup cleaved red onion

- 1 fed or omega3 egg, beaten

- 1 tablespoon coconut flour

Directions:

1. In a huge dry pan, toast the millet over medium warmth for around 5 minutes, mixing or shaking regularly, until brilliant dark colored and fragrant. Try not to consume. Gradually include the vegetable stock and salt, being mindful so as not to get scorched from the rising steam. Mix and bring to bubble. Lower the warmth to stew, spread the container, and cook for around 15 minutes, until all the water is assimilated.

2. Expel from the warmth and let stand secured for 10 minutes, then lighten with a fork. Then, place the onion, carrots, basil, mushrooms, garlic, and Italian flavoring in a nourishment processor fitted with the Sedge and heartbeat into fine pieces.

3. Spot 1 tablespoon of the oil in an enormous skillet over medium warmth, include the

vegetable blend, and sauté for 3 to 4, minutes, until delicate. Move to an enormous bowl. Wipe the skillet clean with a paper towel. Include the millet, beaten egg, and coconut flour to the blending bowl. Mix to join and thicken.

4. With lubed hands, structure the blend into 2inch balls, and afterward push down with the palm of your hand to shape into 12 patties. Include the staying 1 tablespoon oil to the skillet. Include the patties and sauté over medium warmth for 5 minutes for each side. Channel on a papertowelsecured plate before serving.

Shaved Kohlrabi with Crispy Pear and Nuts

Ingredients:

- 1 tablespoon crisp lemon juice

- 1 tablespoon white balsamic vinegar

- Fit salt

- 1/2 cup torn crisp mint leaves, in addition to extra for serving

- 1 tablespoon extravirgin olive oil

- 1/2 cup whitened hazelnuts, pecans, macadamia nuts, or pistachios

- 2 medium kohlrabi, stripped and ground

- 1 fresh pear [Comice. Bosc, or Anjou], cored and ground

- 1/2 teaspoon finely ground lemon pizzazz

- 2 ounces Pecorino de Fossa or Parmigiano Reggiano cheddar, shaved

Directions:

1. Warmth the broiler to 350°F. On a heating sheet, toast the nuts for 10 to 12 minutes, hurling at times, until brilliant dark colored. Cool and coarsely hack. In the meantime, hurl the kohlrabi, pear, lemon get-up-and-go, lemon juice, and vinegar in a bowl.

2. Season with legitimate salt. Include the 1/2 cup mint leaves and hurl to consolidate. Put the toasted nuts in a little bowl and hurl with the olive oil to cover. Season with increasingly salt, if wanted. To serve, isolate the plate of mixed greens among four plates and top with prepared nuts, cheddar, and increasingly mint.

3. MAKE THE CURRY. Warmth the coconut oil on medium high warmth. Include the carrot and cook around 3 minutes, until it just starts to

soften. Turn the warmth down to medium, include the broccoli, onion, and ginger, and cook until they start to soften and dark colored, around 5 minutes. Include the yellow curry powder and cook 1 moment. Then include the coconut drain and salt, blending to blend well.

4. Raise the warmth to medium high again and heat to the point of boiling. Turn the warmth down to medium—low and stew for 15 minutes, mixing at times, until the sauce starts to thicken.

5. MAKE THE NOODLES. While the sauce is cooking, heat the coconut oil in a skillet over medium warmth. Include the spiral zed sweet potato noodles, and cook, mixing often, until they simply start to wither, around 10 minutes. Season with salt.

6. To SERVE. Gap the noodles between 3 plates and top with the curry. Or on the other hand

consolidate before serving. Sprinkle with the cilantro and serve.

Perfect Plantain Pancakes

Ingredients:

- 2 teaspoons pure vanilla extract

- 4 to 5 tablespoons extravirgin coconut oil, divided

- ¼ cup Just Like Sugar

- ⅛ teaspoon sea salt, preferably iodized

- 2 large green plantains, peeled and cut in pieces

- 4 large pastured or omega3 eggs

- ½ teaspoon baking soda

Directions:

1. Place the plantain pieces in a blender or food processor and purée—you should have about

2 cups. Add the eggs and blend to form a smooth batter.

2. Add the vanilla extract, 3 tablespoons of melted coconut oil, Just Like Sugar, the salt, and baking soda. Process on high for 2 to 3 minutes, until smooth.

3. Heat 1 tablespoon coconut oil in a pan or griddle over medium heat. When the oil shimmers, fill a ½ cup measure with batter and pour into the pan. Repeat for two to 4 more pancakes.

4. Cook 4 to 5 minutes, until the top looks fairly dry and has little bubbles. Flip and cook 1½ to 2 minutes more. Repeat with remaining batter, adding more oil as needed.

Paradox Crackers

Ingredients:

- 1 cup almond flour

- ½ cup coconut flour

- ½ teaspoon sea salt, preferably iodized

- 2 large pastured or omega3 eggs

- 1 teaspoon tap or filtered water

- 1 teaspoon Italian seasoning (optional)

Directions:

1. Heat the oven to 350°F. Whisk the eggs and water together in a small bowl.

2. In a medium bowl, mix the almond flour, coconut flour, and salt, adding the Italian seasoning, if desired. Add the egg mixture to

the flour mixture and blend well with a spoon

or spatula, eliminating any lumps.

3. Form into small balls about the size of a large

marble, place on a cookie sheet, press flat

with the back of a fork, and bake for about 20

minutes, until crisp.

4. Let cool on a baking rack before serving.

Carrot Soup

Ingredients:

- Four cloves of garlic (smashed)

- 3 tsps. of cumin seeds

- Four cups of vegetable stock

- 3 tbsps. of olive oil

- Four hundred grams of carrots (cut in disks of 1inch)

- 1 onion (diced)

- 3 bay leaves

- tsp. of salt

- fourth tsp. of white pepper

- 3 tsps. of hy

- fourth cup of yogurt

Directions:

1. Take a heavy bottom pan and add oil in it. Add onions, garlic, and cumin to the pan. Sauté on a medium flame for 7 minutes until tender and golden in color. Stir occasionally.

2. Add the stock, carrots, salt, bay leaves, white pepper, and simmer the mixture. Cover the pan and simmer for twenty minutes.

3. Allow the soup to cool down for five minutes.

4. Use an immersion blender for blending the soup. Blend until you reach a silky smooth consistency.

5. Return the soup to heat and add hy. Stir the soup. Add yogurt and simmer.

6. Taste the soup and adjust the seasonings. Keep the soup warm on very low flame until you serve.

7. Divide the soup among serving bowls. Serve with a dollop of yogurt from the top.

Celery Soup

Ingredients:

- 2 cup of water

- bay leaf

- tsp. of salt

- 1 tsp. of pepper

- third tsp. of cayenne

- 1 cup of sour cream

- fourth cup of each

- 3 tbsps. of olive oil

- 2 onion (diced)

- Four cloves of garlic (chopped)

- 7 cups of celery (thinly sliced)

- 3 cups of potatoes (sliced in rounds)

- Four cups of vegetable stock

- Parsley (small stems)

- Dill (small stems)

Directions:

1. Take a large pot and add oil in it. Heat the oil and start adding the onion. Cook for five minutes until golden.

2. Roughly chop celery, potatoes, and garlic. Add garlic and cook the mixture for 3 minutes. Add potatoes, celery, stock, bay leaf, water, salt, cayenne, and pepper. The liquid needs to be enough to cover the vegetables. Cover the pot and boil the mixture. Simmer for ten minutes.

3. Remove bay leaf after turning off the stove. Add herbs to the pot and allow them to wilt.

4. Take an immersion blender and start blending the soup until silky smooth.

5. Return the pot to heat and cook over low flame for five minutes.

6. Serve with sour cream from the top.

Tomato Soup And Hallowmas Croutons

Ingredients:

- third cup of oil

- Four cups of vegetable stock

- fourth cup of basil leaves (chopped)

- cup of Greek yogurt

- 4 pounds of tomatoes

- 1 red onion (sliced in thin rings)

- 7 cloves of garlic

- 3 tsps. of thyme leaves

For croutons:

- Block of halloo cheese (cut in cubes of 4fourth inch)

- Tbsp. Of oil

Directions:

1. Start by preheating your oven at 200 degrees Celsius.

2. Use parchment paper for lining baking sheet. Spread the onions, tomatoes, and garlic on the sheet. Drizzle with some oil from the top—roast in the oven for thirty minutes.

3. Heat some oil in a pan and start adding the halloo cubes. Cook for four minutes until golden on all sides.

4. Add the roasted veggies in a pot along with the vegetable stock. Use an immersion blender for blending the soup until smooth. Place the pot over a low flame and add seasonings of your choice. Simmer the soup and add basil. Simmer for ten minutes.

5. Add 1 a cup of yogurt to the soup.

6. Serve the soup in serving bowls with croutons from the top.

<h1 style="text-align:center">Chocolate Buckwheat Granola Bars</h1>

Ingredients:

- 1 tablespoon of cocoa powder

- 1 teaspoon of allnatural vanilla extract (i used my homemade)

- 3 tablespoons of date syrup or maple syrup

- 1⅓ cup of buckwheat groats

- 2 bananas

- ¼ cup of peanut butter (or almond butter)

- ⅓ ½ cup of dark chocolate chunks (sweetened with healthy sweeteners if you can find it or you can use unsweetened and

- Increase the date syrup by 1 tablespoon)

Directions:

1. Preheat the oven to 360 degrees F (180
    degrees Celsius).

2. Combine and mash the bananas with peanut
    butter, cocoa powder, vanilla extract and date
    syrup in a bowl.

3. Add chocolate and buckwheat groats and
    pour into a brownie pan.

4. Bake for about 20 minutes until the granola
    bars firm up then set it aside to cool. Enjoy.

Cauliflower Chocolate Pudding

Ingredients:

- 1/3 cup of cacao powder

- 10 pitted Midol dates

- 3 cups of cauliflower florets

- 2 cups of nondairy milk (e.g. almond milk)

- ½ teaspoon of vanilla bean powder (or a teaspoon of vanilla extract)

Directions:

1. Steam the cauliflower until they become tender.
2. Combine all INGREDIENTS: in a blender until smooth and creamy.
3. You can consume immediately or store in the fridge.

Spicy Vegan Black Bean Brownies

Ingredients:

- 1 teaspoon of finely ground sea salt

- 2 teaspoons (5 g) of ground cinnamon

- ½ teaspoon cayenne powder (optional)

- 30 ounces (878 g) of cooked black beans, drained and rinsed well

- 1 cup (240 ml) of pure maple syrup

- 2 teaspoon (10 ml) of pure vanilla extract

- 2 tablespoons of ground flax seed plus 6 tablespoons of water, mixed well

- 1 cup (132 g) oat flour

- 1¼ cup (141 g) cacao or unsweetened cocoa powder

- 1 teaspoon of baking powder

- ¼ (60 ml) cup water, add more by the teaspoon if needed.

Directions:

1. Preheat the oven to 350°F (176°C) and grease a pan to make the flax eggs and let sit.

2. Add the oats, cocoa powder, baking powder, salt, cinnamon, and cayenne pepper to the food processor and grind the oats into flour.

3. Once this has been d, add in the beans, flax eggs, maple syrup, vanilla, and water and process until the batter is smooth and creamy. Use water to thin the mixture as desired.

4. Bake for 1 an hour and let it cool on a rack.

Vacation Oven Roasted Seitan

Ingredients:

- 1 tsp sea salt.

- 1/4 teaspoon dried sage.

- 1 tbsp vegan Worcestershire sauce.

- 1 tbsp sugar complimentary BBQ Sauce.

- 2 tbsp liquid amino (or soy sauce).

- 1 cup Vegetable Broth.

- 1 cup of vital wheat gluten.

- 3 tbsp nutritional yeast.

- 1 tsp smoked paprika.

- 1 tsp dried thyme or 1 fresh spring thyme.

- 1 tsp dried rosemary.

- 1 tbsp garlic powder.

- 4 cups of Vegetable Broth to simmer the
  seitan in.

Directions:

1. Mix together your dry active INGREDIENTS: in
   one bowl and your wet compnts in a second
   bowl.
2. Combine the wet with the dry and knead into
   a "dough".
3. Knead this dough for about 5 minutes or till
   the gluten is activated.
4. Bring about 4 cups of veggie broth to a
   simmer on mediumhigh.
5. The majority of dishes require you to wrap
   your seitan in plastic wrap prior to simmering,
   but that's only to keep the shape, and we
   discover that we like ours rustic and loaded
   with vegetable broth flavor.

6. Simply roll your seitan dough into a log and simmer in the covered pot of vegetable broth for 45 minutes.

7. After 45 minutes preheat your oven to 350° F and bake the seitan on a baking tray for 20 minutes, flipping it after 10 minutes.

Chickpea Tofu With Tahini Sauce

Ingredients:

For the chickpea tofu:

- 1/2 tsp garlic powder.

- 1 tsp freshly ground black pepper.

- 1/4 tsp cayenne pepper.

- 1 tbsp coconut oil or olive oil.

- 1 1/2 tsp salt.

- 2 cups garbanzo bean flour.

- 1/4 cup dietary yeast.

- 2 tsp ground cumin.

For the tahini sauce:

- 1 tsp apple cider vinegar.

- Newly ground black pepper.

- 1 tbsp black sesame seeds.

- 1/4 cup tahini.

- 1 clove garlic, minced.

Directions:

1. Preheat the oven to 400° F. in a big bowl, combine all the chickpea tofu components with 3/4 cup of water and mix well.

2. Line a baking pan with parchment paper, and gather the batter.

3. Bake for 20 minutes, or up until a toothpick inserted into the center comes out tidy.

4. Eliminate from the oven, let cool totally and cut into bitesize pieces.

5. In a separate bowl, mix together the tahini sauce active ingredients and 2 tablespoons of water (add more water if the tahini is too thick).

6. Serve the chickpea tofu on a bed of arugula,
   topped with the tahini sauce.

Korean Braised Tofu

Ingredients:

- 1/2 1 tbsp Korean chili powder.

- 3 tbsp soy sauce.

- 4 tbsp sake.

- 1 scallion, cut into thin slices.

- 1 onion, cut into thin pieces.

- 1 14ounce block firm tofu, cut into 16 squares.

- 1 tbs sugar.

- Toasted sesame seeds.

Directions:

1. Location onion slices on a nonstick skillet or frying pan, then leading with pieces of tofu.

2. Mix sugar, Korean chili powder, soy sauce, and sake together. Put over tofu slices.

3. Cover the frying pan with a lid. Turn the heat to high and cook until boiling. Turn the heat to mediumhigh, and cook for another 5 minutes, baste with the sauce a number of times.

4. Remove lid, turn the heat back to high, and cook till the sauce has actually minimized.

5. Shut off heat, transfer to a serving plate, garnish with scallions and sesame seeds. Serve immediately.

Sunshine Smoothie

Ingredients:

- 200g pineapple (canned or fresh)

- 3 bananas, broken into chunks

- Little piece ginger, peeled

- 500ml lettuce juice, chilled

- 20g cashew nuts juice lime

Directions:

1. Place The INGREDIENTS: at a blender and whizz until smooth.
2. Drink directly away or pour into a jar to drink on the move. Will keep in the refrigerator for a single day.

Vegan Smoothie

Ingredients:

- 200ml (1/2 tall glass) unsweetened soya milk

- 1 cherry soya yogurt

- 3 tablespoons or 50g firm silken tofu

- 75g (1 vacant yogurt kettle) frozen cherry

- 100ml (1/4 tall glass) cherry

- Juice (we utilized Cherrygood)

- 2 tbsp porridge oat

Directions:

1. Quantify each of the comments just or utilize a tall glass along with your empty yogurt pot for rate they do not need to be precise.

2. Place them in a blender and blitz until
    smooth. Pour 1 tall glass (you will have
    enough to get a high up) or 2 short tumblers.

Kiwi Fruit Smoothie

Ingredients:

- 1 mango, peeled, std and sliced

- 500ml lemon juice

- 3 peeled kiwi berry

- 1 banana, sliced

Directions:

1. Place All the INGREDIENTS: at a blender and blitz until smooth, then pour into 3 tall glasses.

Fudge Brownies

Ingredients:

- Brewed coffee (instant or brewed), 1 tablespoon

- ½ cup of baked sweet potato

- 2 scoops of lectinfree supplement protein powder

- 1 egg

- Baking soda, 1 teaspoon

- Tahini butter, 2 tablespoons

- Sea salt, a pinch, to taste

- Butter or margarine, 2 teaspoons

Directions:

1. Prepare the oven by preheating to 350 degrees and lightly greasing a pan with butter (about 6 x 6 inches). In a medium bowl, mix the sweet potato puree, tahini, egg, supplement protein powder, coffee, baking soda, and sea salt.

2. Combine the INGREDIENTS: with a hand mixer, whisk until the blended INGREDIENTS: are smooth. Using a spatula, remove all batter from the bowl.

3. Place the brownie mix into a baking dish and cook for approximately 2022 min.

4. A toothpick should come out clean to confirm the brownies are ready.

5. Remove brownies from heat and allow to cool. Brownies can be served warm or saved in a seals container at room temp for 4 days, or the refrigerator for week.

6. Brownies can be frozen for longer, though they should be returned to room temperature or warmed to serve, for best results.

Macadamia Nut Chocolate Cookies

Ingredients:

- 1 egg

- Brewed coffee, 2 tablespoons

- Vanilla extract, 1 tablespoon

- Yacon sweetener or monk fruit syrup, 1 tablespoon

- Hy, raw, 1 teaspoon

- Baking soda, ½ teaspoon

- 1 scoop of supplement powder, protein, lectinfree

- Sweet potatoes, ½ baked and mashed

- Dark chocolate chips, unsweetened or semisweet, ¼ cup (plus more for a topping)

- Tahini, 2 tablespoons

- Whole macadamia nuts, ¼ cups

Directions:

1. Combine the following INGREDIENTS: in a mediumsized bowl: sweet potato, tahini, egg, coffee, supplement protein, yacon or monk fruit syrup (or stevia), hy, and baking soda.

2. Mix the INGREDIENTS: using an electric mixer until the mixture is blended well, and the texture is smooth and creamy.

3. Fold in the chocolate chips and make sure they are at least 75% cocoa. Use a spatula or wooden spoon to mix the chocolate chips well into the mix.

4. Prepare the oven by preheating to 350 degrees, then line a baking tray for cookies with a silic mat or parchment paper.

5. Take note that this cookie batter is sticky, and the parchment paper or mat will need to be

evenly greased (lightly) with butter or olive oil before setting the cookie dough portions on the tray.

6. Place a dollop or portion of the batter on the sheet, and continue, spacing them apart by 12 inches, and press them down gently in the center to flatten them into a circle.

7. Press the macadamia nuts into each cookie, distributing them evenly.

8. Sprinkle more chocolate chips onto each cookie, in between the macadamia nuts on top.

9. Bake the cookies for 1012 minutes, then remove to cool on the tray first, then enjoy. For best results, place the cookies on a wire rack to cool completely.

Chia Seed Pudding

Ingredients:

- 1 ½ cups of coconut milk

- 2 tablespoons of monk fruit, stevia or another low carb sweetener

- Vanilla extract, 1 teaspoon

- ½ cup of chia seeds (any variety – red, black or brown seeds)

- ½ cup of coconut or dairy cream (full fat cream)

- Cinnamon for topping

Directions:

1. Combine the cream, coconut milk, and vanilla extract into a medium bowl and whisk together.

2. Add in the monk fruit or natural sweetener, along with the chia seeds.

3. Continue to stir well until all INGREDIENTS: are thoroughly blended. If desired, add a small amount of cinnamon into the pudding mix, or reserve to top later.

4. Pour the mixture into a sealable container and place in the refrigerator for 3 hours, or overnight.

5. This will allow the chia to thicken or gel together with the milk and other INGREDIENTS: and create the pudding.

Paradox Cappuccino

Ingredients:

- 1 tablespoon MCT oil

- 1 tablespoon of grassfed butter or goat butter

- 1 cup hot coffee

- 1 pack of stevia

Directions:

1. Place the INGREDIENTS: in a mixer for 30 seconds.

2. Put it into a mug and serve your cappuccino.

3. That's it!

Tops And Bottoms Celery Soup

Ingredients:

- 1/2 of chopped red onion

- 1 tablespoon of chopped rosemary leaves

- 1/2 teaspoon sea salt

- 1/2 teaspoon black pepper

- 3 cups of vegetable broth

- 3 tablespoons of olive oil (avocado oil also works)

- 1pound of peeled and cut celery root

- 2 celery stems with leaves, cut into small pieces

- 1/2 lemon juice

Directions:

1. In a heavy saucepan on medium heat, heat the 3 tablespoons of olive oil, and then add chopped celery root, celery leaves, onion, rosemary and salt, and pepper.
2. Cook for 5 minutes until de celery roots start to soften.
3. Now you can add the broth and lemon until it boils.
4. At this point reduce the heat, cover the mix and let it simmer for 1 an hour.
5. Stir once in a while and check if the celery root is soft.
6. Once it is tender, remove the soup from the stove.
7. Pass 1 of the soup to a blender and blend it until it's creamy.
8. Repeat with the rest and reheat the whole soup in the saucepan for another 5 minutes.
9. You're good to serve.

Raw Mushroom Soup

Ingredients:

- 1/2 teaspoon of sea salt

- 1/4 teaspoon of black pepper

- 2 fresh thyme leaves

- 1 tablespoon truffle oil

- 2 ½ cups of your preferred mushrooms

- 1/2 cup almond butter

- 1 tablespoon dried onion or 3 tablespoons of sliced red onion

Directions:

1. Cut 1/2 cup of the mushrooms and set aside.

2. Then, put the other 2 cups of mushrooms, the water, almond butter, onions, salt, pepper, and thyme in a food processor.

3. Process high for 30 seconds, and then blend for 2 minutes.

4. Check the temperature as it should be just warm.

5. If you want it to be hotter you can blend for another minute.

6. The texture should be somewhat gravylike.

7. Serve in a bowl and top with the rest of the diced mushrooms and sprinkle with the truffle oil.

Holiday Muffins

Ingredients:

- Pinch of ground cloves

- Pinch of nutmeg

- ½ teaspoon ground cinnamon

- ¾ teaspoon baking soda

- 1 cup fresh blueberries

- 1/3 cup homemade pumpkin puree

- 2 ½ cups almond flour

- 1 teaspoon apple cider vinegar

- 2 tablespoons organic hy

- 2 tablespoons coconut oil, melted

- 3 large organic eggs

- ¼ teaspoon salt

- 1 teaspoon organic vanilla extract

Directions:

1. Preheat the oven to 350°Fahrenheit. Line cups of muffin tin with paper liners.
2. In a mixing bowl, mix baking soda, flour, spices and salt.
3. In another bowl, add coconut oil, eggs, hy, vinegar and vanilla extract and mix well.
4. Add pumpkin puree and beat well to combine.
5. Add the egg mixture to flour mixture and mix well.
6. Gently, fold in blueberries.
7. Place the mixture into prepared muffin cups.
8. Bake for 18 minutes.
9. Remove from your oven and keep on wire rack to cool for about 5 minutes.
10. Carefully, invert the muffins onto wire rack to completely cool before serving.

Carrot Bread

Ingredients:

- ¼ teaspoon salt

- ¼ teaspoon salt

- 1 teaspoon ground cinnamon

- 1 teaspoon baking soda

- 1 teaspoon organic baking powder

- 2 tablespoons coconut flour

- 2 cups almond flour

- ½ cup carrot, peeled and shredded

- 1/3 cup coconut oil, melted

- 1/3 cup organic hy

- 3 organic eggs

- ¼ cup walnuts, chopped

Directions:

1. Preheat the oven to 325°Fahrenheit. Grease a loaf pan.
2. In mixing bowl, add baking soda, baking powder, flour, cinnamon and salt.
3. In another bowl, mix eggs, coconut oil, hy and carrot and mix well.
4. Add the flour mixture with egg mixture and mix well.
5. Gently, fold in the walnuts.
6. Transfer the mixture to prepared loaf pan.
7. Bake for about 38 minutes. Add to a wire rack to allow to cool for 10 minutes.
8. Invert your bread onto wire rack and slice and serve.

Flourless Bread

Ingredients:

- ½ teaspoon salt

- ¾ teaspoon baking soda

- 1 tablespoon apple cider vinegar

- 1 cup cashew butter

- 5 organic eggs

Directions:

1. Preheat the oven to 375°Fahrenheit. Line a loaf pan with parchment paper.
2. Add all of your INGREDIENTS: into food processor and pulse until smooth.
3. Transfer your mixture to a prepared loaf pan.
4. Bake for about 40 minutes.
5. Remove from the oven and keep on a wire rack to cool in pan for about 10 minutes.

6. Invert your bread onto a wire rack and allow it
    to cool for 10 minutes.

7. Slice the bread into desired sized slices and
    serve.

Roasted Beet And Orange Salad

INGREDIENTS:

- 4 medium sized beets, roasted and sliced 2 oranges, peeled and segmented

- 4 cups mixed salad greens

- ½ cup crumbled vegan goat cheese or feta cheese (optional) ¼ cup chopped walnuts or pistachios

- Fresh mint leaves for garnish

For the dressing:

- 2 tablespoons extravirgin olive oil

- 1 tablespoon balsamic vinegar

- 1 teaspoon Dijon mustard

- 1 teaspoon maple syrup or hy

- Salt and pepper to taste

Directions:

1. In a large salad bowl, combine the roasted and sliced beets, orange segments, mixed salad greens, crumbled vegan goat cheese or feta cheese (if using), and chopped walnuts or pistachios.

2. Olive oil, balsamic vinegar, Dijon mustard, maple syrup or hy, salt, and pep per are combined to make the dressing in a small basin.

3. Drizzle the dressing over the salad and toss gently until well coated.

4. Garnish with fresh mint leaves for an extra burst of flavor.

5. Enjoy this vibrant and nutrient packed roasted beet and orange salad as a wholesome and delicious meal.

Summer Berry Spinach Salad

Ingredients:

- 1 cup fresh strawberries, sliced

- 1 cup fresh blueberries

- ½ cup sliced almonds

- 4 cups baby spinach leaves

- ¼ cup crumbled vegan feta cheese (optional)
  Fresh mint leaves for garnish

For the dressing:

- 1 tablespoon balsamic vinegar

- 1 teaspoon Dijon mustard

- 1 teaspoon maple syrup or hy

- 2 tablespoons extra virgin olive oil

- Salt and pepper to taste

Directions:

1. In a large salad bowl, combine the baby spinach leaves, sliced strawberries, blueberries, sliced almonds, and crumbled vegan feta cheese (if using).

2. In a small bowl, whisk together the olive oil, balsamic vinegar, Dijon mustard, maple syrup or hy, salt, and pepper to create the dressing.

3. Drizzle the dressing over the salad and toss gently until well coated.

4. Garnish with fresh mint leaves for an extra burst of freshness.

5. Enjoy this refreshing and colorful summer r berry spinach salad as a delightful side dish or light meal.

Autumn Harvest Sala:

Ingredients:

- ½ cup toasted pecans or walnuts, chopped ¼ cup dried cranberries

- ¼ cup crumbled vegan goat cheese or feta cheese (optional)

- 4 cups mixed salad greens

- 1 cup roasted butternut squash, cubed

- ½ cup pomegranate arils

For the dressing:

- 2 tablespoons extra virgin olive oil

- Salt and pepper to taste

- 2 tablespoons apple cider vinegar

- 1 tablespoon maple syrup or hy

- 1 teaspoon Dijon mustard

Directions:

1. In a large salad bowl, combine the mixed salad greens, roasted butternut squash cubes, pomegranate arils, toasted pecans or walnuts, dried cranberries, and crumbled vegan goat cheese or feta cheese (if using).

2. In a small bowl, whisk together the apple cider vinegar, maple syrup or hy, Dijon mustard, extra virgin olive oil, salt, and pepper to create the dressing.

3. Drizzle the dressing over the salad and toss gently until well combined.

4. Serve this autumn harvest salad as a hearty and flavorsome dish that captures the essence of the season.

Broccoli Puffs

Ingredients:

- 1/2 teaspoon dark pepper

- 1/2 teaspoon your worry up or nearby nectar

- 1 teaspoon iodized ocean salt

- 1 tablespoon minced parsley

- 1/4 cup ground parmesan cheddar or healthful yeast

- 2 cups of broccoli florettes, steamed until delicate

- egg or veggie lover egg

- 1/2 yellow onion, minced

- clove garlic, minced

- 1/2 cup cassava flour

- 1/4 cup whitened almond dinner

- Hot sauce or guacamole for plunging

Directions:

1. Preheat the stove to 400°F. Oil a heating sheet with a slight layer of oil and put in a safe spot.

2. In the work chunk of a nourishment processor fitted with a Ssharp edge, beat the broccoli, eggs, onion, garlic, cassava flour, almond milk, pepper, syrup or nectar, salt, parsley, and cheddar or yeast.

3. Scoop around 1/2 tablespoons of blend and delicately squeezed between your hands to frame a potato tot shape.

4. Wash your hands between each couple of tots to forestall staying. Spot the tights on the heating sheet, equally divided.

5. Heat for in any event 10 to 20 minutes, or until brilliant darker. Present with hot sauce or guacamole if wanted.

6. It's fine to utilize a fast blender, similar to a vita blend, as well. Simply work in groups, taking consideration not to pack, because the blend can stall out in the base and get over a mixed and turn soft.

Prepared "Singed" Artichoke Hearts

Ingredients:

- 1/8 teaspoon cayenne pepper powder

- 10 solidified artichoke hearts. defrosted and tapped dry with paper towels

- 1 cup almond. coconut, or cassava flour

- 1/4 teaspoon ocean salt, ideally iodized, in addition to extra for serving

- 1/4 teaspoon split dark pepper

- 4 tablespoons extra virgin olive oil [or perils oil]

- Juice of 1/2 lemon, or 2 tablespoons packaged lemon juice

- Lemon wedges

Directions:

1. Warmth the broiler to 400°F. Spot 3 tablespoons of the olive oil, the lemon juice, and cayenne pepper in a blending bowl and speed until mixed.

2. Add the artichoke hearts to the bowl and mix until very much covered.

3. Coat a rimmed heating sheet with the staying 1 tablespoon olive oil.

4. Spot the flour, the 1/4 teaspoon salt, and the pepper in a 1 quart resalable plastic sack.

5. Utilizing tongs or your hands, add the artichokes to the sack and shake to gently cover.

6. On the other hand, blend the flour, the 1/4 teaspoon salt, and the pepper in a glass dish with a tight fitting cover. Include the artichokes and, holding the top immovably, shake to cover.

7. Spot the artichoke hearts on the heating sheet and prepare for 20 to 25 minutes, turning the artichokes or shaking the dish a few times, until the artichokes are brilliant dark colored and firm.

8. Expel to a serving dish, sprinkle with progressively salt, if wanted, and present with lemon wedges.

Veggie Curry With Sweet Potato "Noodles"

Ingredients:

Curry

- 1/3 cup hacked onion, or 2 tablespoons dried minced onion

- 1 teaspoon minced new ginger, or 1/2 teaspoon dried ginger

- 1 tablespoon yellow curry powder

- 13.5ounce without bpa can fullfat coconut milk or coconut cream

- Squeeze ocean salt, ideally iodized

- 1/2 tablespoon extravirgin coconut oil

- 1 huge carrot, spiralized or julienned

- 1 cup broccoli, cut into scaled down pieces

Sweet potato "noodles"

- 1/2 tablespoon coconut oil

- 1 huge sweet potato, stripped and spiralized with the 3mm cutting edge

- Squeeze salt

- 4 tablespoons hacked cilantro or level leaf parsley, for embellish

Directions:

1. MAKE THE CURRY. Warmth the coconut oil on medium

2. high warmth. Include the carrot and cook around 3 minutes, until it just starts to soften. Turn the warmth down to medium, include the broccoli, onion, and ginger, and cook until they start to soften and dark colored, around 5 minutes. Include the yellow curry powder and cook 1 moment. Then include the coconut drain and salt, mixing to blend well.

3. Raise the warmth to medium high again and heat to the point of boiling. Turn the warmth down to medium low and stew for 15 minutes, blending incidentally, until the sauce starts to thicken.

4. MAKE THE NOODLES. While the sauce is cooking, heat the coconut oil in a skillet over medium warmth. Include the spiral zed sweet potato noodles, and cook, blending often, until they simply start to shrink, around 10 minutes. Season with salt.

5. To SERVE. Separation the noodles between 3 plates and top with the curry. Or on the other hand join before serving. Sprinkle with the cilantro and serve.